CW00327331

dear me,

letters to my pregnant self

Published by Vicki Smith on behalf of Connexions Leicester Shire

Compilation © Connexions Leicester Shire 2010

Contributions © Individual copyright holders

ISBN: 978-1-907540-07-3

Dear You,

The idea of becoming a young mum or dad can be scary. It is likely that as a pregnant teenager and as a young parent you will experience challenging situations and face discrimination in one form or another. But life doesn't end when you become a young parent and neither do your hopes and dreams.

Through this book we hope to provide inspiration to pregnant teenagers and young parents, to offer hope and reassurance that there are still many opportunities out there.

The gift of hindsight would be an incredible thing! Through this project, participants have had the opportunity to share some of the lessons they have learned with young people who are in a similar situation now.

A big thank you to all of the people who have written letters for this book. You are living proof that young parents can cope with the challenges that they might face and live happy and fulfilled lives.

Love from Us x

Dear Susan,

You have now told everybody you know that you are pregnant. They have mostly responded with cries of delight. A few women have said things like, "now your troubles begin", or "you'll not have a good night's sleep until the kid leaves home".

You have accepted the congratulations and the witch's warnings with your usual guarded smile.

You have not told anybody that you are terrified. You were married one week after your 18th birthday and you are still a child. You have never held a newborn baby and have no idea of how to look after such a fragile creature. There is nobody in the world you can talk to about your true feelings.

You must leave your job at the BP petrol station where you work, sitting in a little glass box on the forecourt, and somehow managing to read a Penguin paperback a day between filling tanks. Your doctor thinks that the petrol fumes could harm your baby. You find work in a printing firm packing cardboard Bird's Eye display units. One lunchtime you are discovered reading The Guardian by the manager and are instantly promoted to a colour matcher on the printing floor. You have not told the manager that you are pregnant. The smell of the hot ink and the fumes mean that you cannot stay. You leave and the manager is furious and disappointed.

Meanwhile the baby is growing and kicking. Your young husband likes to place his hand on your swollen belly and feel the baby communicating through your skin. You don't tell him that you don't want this baby.

You spend the next few months growing out of your own clothes and into somebody else's. You stop being Susan Townsend and become an anonymous pregnant woman. You walk round in maternity tents, your hormones are rioting like prisoners in a high security unit, they force you to eat a dozen oranges a day and to tramp around the city streets surrounding your flat on a search for beauty – you need to see trees and flowers, even weeds excite you – you feel you are seeing these natural things for the first time. You long for the countryside.

On the 10th July 1965 your waters break. Your baby is six weeks premature. After an agonizing half an hour he is born. He weighs two pounds and thirteen ounces and is transparent, his veins and arteries are visible. He fits into your hand. The Irish midwife tells you that he won't live. She says that he should be christened before he dies.

The book you have taken to the hospital with you is I knock at the Door by Seán O'Casey. I call the baby Sean. The nurse mutters a prayer and with her index finger makes the sign of the cross on my tiny son's forehead. Then we are parted. He goes to the premature baby unit in an incubator and I am taken downstairs to a ward. I lie awake trying to work out if I will be able to love this little child.

Then the thunder starts, it rattles the windows. The rain falls like a monsoon. Violent lightening illuminates the other women on the ward, some of them stir and sit up. I start to cry, not because I am afraid of the storm – I have always loved the drama of bad weather – I tell the nurse that I must go to the Premature Baby Unit. I explain that my son is in there and he will almost certainly be afraid of the storm. I sob that I have to go upstairs to protect him.

Now and always.

Sue Townsend was born in Leicester in 1946. At the age of thirty-five, she won the Thames Television Playwright Award for her play Womberang (published in Bazaar and Rummage, 1984) and started her writing career. Other plays followed including The Great Celestial Cow (1984), Ten Tiny Fingers, Nine Tiny Toes (1990), and most recently Are You Sitting Comfortably? but she has become most well-known for her series of books about Adrian Mole.

The first of Adrian Mole book, The Secret Diary of Adrian Mole aged 13¾ was published in 1982 and was followed by The Growing Pains of Adrian Mole (1984). These two books made her the best-selling novelist of the 1980s. They have been followed by several more in the same series including Adrian Mole: The Wilderness Years (1993), and Adrian Mole and the Weapons of Mass Destruction (2004). The books have been adapted for radio, television and theatre.

In 2001, Sue wrote The Public Confessions of a Middle-Aged Woman aged 55¾ (2001), a collection of monthly columns written for Sainsbury's magazine from 1993-2001. Leicester University awarded her an Honorary MA in 1991.

Sue's most recent Mole is Adrian Mole: The Prostrate Years (Michael Joseph 2009).

Dear Dee (19 years)

This is the happiest time of your life, when you had Jasmine everything made sense at last and you felt so much happiness and love for Jasmine, something that you hadn't ever felt before. I know that you are scared too. Finding a house, a career, sorting money out just seems totally impossible right now and you don't have anyone to help, not that you would accept it anyway.

So, here it is, a list of things to get you through until you are 30, after that I have no idea, I am still learning!

* Don't stay in a relationship that makes you unhappy, if you know it isn't forever and it makes you feel horrible - get out and don't look back!

* It is impossible to be a perfect mum, anything less and you beat yourself up to the point you don't sleep - babies need love, milk and warmth and a bit more love just to make sure. Just relax and enjoy it - when Grandmama says it flies by and before you know it they are grown up she is right! Take lots and lots of photos too, you will never get bored of looking at them.

* Pay your bills, pay your bills, and pay your bills!

* Forget the friends that weren't friends and just focus on the few people that really do care. You may not see them all the time but they will eventually see you through.

* When you accept that council flat they offer, with the boarded up window and purple walls, take it and trust me you will make it home , buy it off the council and this will be you and Jasmine's first proper home where you feel safe. Don't cry, buy paint and get on with it!

* Stop worrying about how you are going to find a job, it will come to you - you feel passionately that young parents need support not criticism and eventually you will make this your career. Do what you love; work hard and it will be fine!

* Go to the stay and plays and the health visitor clinics, if older mums aren't so friendly then don't worry about it. You want to go and have fun with Jasmine, don't let anyone put you off. You have as much right as them to be there.

* Accept help when it is offered, stop being so stubborn. Just because you need a bit of support now and then doesn't mean you can't cope. No one will think badly of you.

* You are not your mother - keep reading the parenting books and then make up your own mind. Use your common sense and instincts. Jasmine is amazing and will shine with your love!

* Learn to cook and stop buying food from Iceland. Buy a student cook book and learn the basics first and you will begin to love it. It will save you loads of money and Jasmine will love to cook with you when she is older.

Everything will be OK, life is full of up and downs but you and Jasmine will be ok!

Lots of love

Dee (30 years)

P.S You will have beautiful little boy when you are 27. You will think you can't love anyone as much as Jasmine but you will.

Dear Teenage Pregnant Me,

I wasn't sure how to begin this letter, or what I should say. I wanted to offer some pearls of wisdom, some kind of brilliant insight that would inspire you, assure that everything will turn out OK. But actually, I think you already know that.

One of the things I most admire about you, and something I know your friends and family love you for, is your amazing (sometimes annoying!) ability to see the positive in everything. At 16, the world seems so simple, and you are enviously laid back about having a baby and how it will fit into your life.

Of course you were shocked at first to find out you were pregnant, and I'm sure you are a bit scared deep down, but above all you have that amazing adaptability and resilience that comes with youth. A can do attitude that won't take no for an answer. You're studying for your A-levels at the moment and why on earth should being eight and a half months pregnant stop you sitting a few exams? Too right. Don't let anyone tell you that being a teenage mum automatically leaves you on the educational scrapheap.

I guess what I want to say is that I'm proud of you. Right now, carrying on as normal comes naturally to you, and you are oblivious to anyone looking or judging you. Being pregnant just means you have more time for revision. As you get older though, and your aspirations and ambitions push you through all kinds of obstacles, I hope you appreciate just how fantastic you are - both as an individual, successful in your own right, and as a role model for your children. When they look at you they will see a woman who has the strength to pursue her dreams, whatever life might put in her way.

Cherish your family and friends - you are going to need their support and when you need them most they will be there for you.

There will of course be times when being a mum will limit your options. You may even feel resentful at times when you see your friends with no responsibilities, out every night, or travelling the world. But remember that being a mum doesn't mean you can't be a person, it doesn't mean you can't do all the things you ever believed you would. You are about to have a baby, but you can be everything you want to be.

Jo Middleton is a freelance journalist and mother of two, living in Somerset. Pregnant at 16, she had her first baby in the summer holidays between the first and second year of her A-levels and went on to get a first class economics degree. Now 31, Jo is a proud mum to two daughters - Bee, aged 14, and Belle, aged 7.

Dear Katie (aged 17)

Well you have just found out you're pregnant. You're feeling worried about the future, nervous about telling people, concerned about somewhere to live, work, money, there is a lot to think about and you are not sure of the answers right now. Well I'm writing to you from seven years down the line to send you advice from lessons learnt... listen to this advice it will help!

* You may be worried at first, but it's OK, your son will be the making of you, he will grow into an amazing boy that you will be so proud of! He is the child you will want to change the world for and give him everything you can.

* Don't be scared of asking for help when its needed, this doesn't make you weak it makes you real.

* Don't always listen to others 'advice' they don't always know best!

* Your first home will be on a non desirable estate, no you don't want your son to grow up here but don't worry you won't be there forever.

* Throw out the micro meals and learn to cook, you might actually enjoy it!!

* Keep going to the groups that you want to go to, ignore the older mums looking down on you, you have just as much right to be there, rise above it, you are there for your son.

* If you're not sure of someone then trust your instincts, you are not wrong! Avoid! This also goes for relationships, don't waste time trying to make a wrong thing right, just keep going Mr Right will come to you.

* Attend the young parents group your midwife tells you about, this will make you realise you want to work with other young parents, this wanting will lead to an amazing career which you'll love.

* You'll go through times of thinking life is going nowhere, well this certainly isn't the case, life is just beginning you just can't see it yet, you'll meet an amazing man who'll love you and your son the way you both deserve, he would give you the earth if he could, he will bring out the best in you and together you will reach for the stars.
You'll decide to move away together this is the fresh start you'll be longing for, you'll buy a house which the three of you will make your lovely home, you will marry this man in a wedding beyond your wildest dreams, you'll also visit places you never dreamt of (honestly this will all happen as much as you don't think that yet!)

* You'll go through times of wondering who you are, well you will find you are a determined, tattooed, red head, making the most of life and loving it — yes that is very different to who you are right now!

* You will get through the next few years, even though at times it does seem very hard, and you know what? When you get on the other side you'll appreciate it even more because of the bad times, don't waste time beating yourself up over what you couldn't change, life is amazing. Make the most of every opportunity.

Well that's some advice that'll help you through the next few years, and after that.... who knows? The adventure continues......

Lots of love

Katie (age 23)

Hey you!

Now I know things are dark at the moment and you are feeling lost, a lot of stuff has happened so far in your life, and it is all about to change!

In October 1998 you will discover you are pregnant and it will feel so right. The relationship may not be the best but all of that will sort itself out in time.

Mum and Dad will be fine, well Dad will be shocked, but what did you expect!

The pregnancy will be hard, but the birth will be the best thing ever! And when you first lay your eyes on your beautiful daughter Olivia nothing in the world will matter.

There will be hard times and you may feel that you're not doing a good enough job and some people will be judgemental, sod them they don't know what a fab mum you are. Be sure of yourself, its all fine.

You will fall for someone else and have another baby. The relationship will not be the best but you will learn many lessons and once again that baby, Carys, will be so worth it! (She's crazy, in the best possible way!!)

You will find that special man, and believe me he's worth the wait! Another baby will enter the world and be the icing on your beautiful cake!

A lot of ups and downs, heartache and happiness. It's not anything like you thought it would be and thank the lord it wasn't, its been interesting to say the least and you won't want to change a thing!

Just a few tips though:

Go to college you will NEVER regret it!

When you and Dee don't speak for a while, don't worry you'll work it out and it will be the best friendship ever! (She will still be a really bad singer, but hey, pro's and con's baby, pro's and con's)

Really don't be bothered by what narrowed minded people say just hold your head up high and keep loving those babies!

Be more confident and trust your instincts.

Keep laughing at yourself!!!

Loadsa Love your 30 yr old self (and yes you will actually be 30 one day!)

P.s Do your pelvic floor exercises! Your bladder will suffer!!

Dear Suzannah

I know your life is really tough for you at the moment, you don't know whether you're coming or going with home life. The next two years are just going to get harder, try and focus on your education because you're not stupid even if people make out you are. You're going to make mistakes but try not to let others tell you what to do because you will end up getting yourself into trouble with the law.

You will always think of your mum but believe me you will get over her because it wasn't your fault her walking out on you, as I know your blaming yourself for it happening, but after a while things will start to look up. You will meet a guy and you will fall in love with him, but you need to keep your wits about you as you will get hurt along the line more than once, but you will get pregnant even if the first time you do mother nature will take the pregnancy away from you and you will be hurt and upset. You will soon fall pregnant again and you will have the most gorgeous little baby girl ever, it will be tough having a baby at 18 but there are so many places that can help and support you, one of them is the PIPS team. Take all the help they offer don't be to proud to take it as it will benefit you in the long run, maybe you might end up working with them who knows? You and your dad will start having a really good relationship, and I know you won't be able to forget what's happened but when he says sorry say it back as he will end up helping you out so much!

If you can try not to get a tattoo on your hand because you will end up hating it, and will cost about £1000 to remove!

Whenever you get down remember this–

Take what life throws at you

Never look back always look forwards

Chin up and smile

Be proud for what you have

It's your life just live it

Always remain true

You will understand this when you're 19,

Look after yourself because you might feel that you're worthless at times but you will go on to do amazing things that could help other people in the future

Lots of love
Suzannah (age 19)

Dear Anne-Marie (14 years)

A week before Christmas 2002 you find out you are 5 months pregnant needless to say this is the worst time of your life. You don't know what is going to happen after the initial night of tears, everyone completely understands and starts planning for the future. After all there is no going back now. A week overdue you give birth to the most beautiful little girl you have ever seen. A healthy 7lb 13oz, her name is Emily Jane. The bond between you is instant, a proper Mummy's girl, she soon becomes the apple of everyone's eyes. You find motherhood a breeze, sleepless nights and dirty nappies comes naturally to you.

The first 2 years of her life you throw yourself into schoolwork (yes you do go back when Emily is 4 months old) and do brilliantly. Although it was hard work it certainly paid off when you finally get your results, with Emily by your side of course. Nobody thought you could do it, especially as you also worked, but you get excellent grades (2 A's, 5 B's and 3 C's). You have proved that whatever life chucks at you, all you need to do is believe in yourself!

After your GCSE exams, you move into your own flat, you think it's perfect! Now it's just you and Emily facing the world. You meet lots of great people and finally feel like an adult.

The following 2 years you continue with your education by attending sixth form and completing your A Levels. You work in various jobs throughout this time, that you never particularly enjoy, but it paid the bills and you are able to provide for yourself and Emily without relying on anyone else. Doing this has set you up for life and changed your attitude for the better. Working is a needs must whether or not you like it! You go on to work full-time at a bank, it is hard work but you thoroughly enjoy it.

Two years after giving birth you finally meet a wonderful man, Stuart, who completely sweeps you off your feet and you fall head over heels in love with him. He takes on your beautiful daughter and showers you both with love and affection. He is perfect for you and treats Emily as his own; they quickly form a bond that will never be broken. You have a gorgeous little girl that you are utterly proud of, life is perfect and nothing will change that.

At the age of 19 you find out you are pregnant for the second time. After the initial shock you are both so overjoyed. This time you could do everything properly. You go on to give birth to the most beautiful little boy you have ever seen. A healthy 8lb 1oz you call him Charlie. His big sister is the happiest little girl ever and takes on being the big sister in her stride. They have a great bond and love each other dearly. You couldn't ask for anything more perfect! You fall into a job when Charlie is 5 months old, it gives you the ideal hours and you thoroughly enjoy it, the best job you have ever had.

Unfortunately your relationship with Stuart doesn't last and you are left on your own. You are now a proud single mother who works hard to provide for Emily and Charlie and have the most incredible bond with both of them. You should be proud of what you have achieved, after all you have had many obstacles to go through but you have always come out the other side with your head held high. You are proof to everyone that whatever life throws at you and whatever your circumstances you can achieve what you want. Don't dwell on the past, what's done is done there is nothing that can change that. Look to the future, after all you have come this far, don't let minor things hold you back.

You have your whole life ahead of you, just remember you are an amazing person and a great Mum, don't ever let anyone try and tell you otherwise!

All my love

Anne-Marie (21years)

So you were a teenage mum! Lacking in experience maybe, but only because they hung on to the knowledge.

From the moment he was born, my responsibility, always and for ever my son.

Never wavering, totally loving, connected, growing together. Opportunistically waiting to be his best winger ever!

So proud I could burst, could've then, could now and every minute in between.

That long journey I now see has taken no time at all, and I am still relishing every single moment of our lives!! x

Beverley

dear a little bit younger me,

you used to be such a partier, drinking and undetermined! but you'll see after having our little man that your life changes so much for the better!!

you will learn love you have never felt before and learn you now have a reason for being in life!

you will get over the fears and insecurities you had before and grow into a strong woman all in one year!

you will be continually amazed everyday at your always developing and growing little man. you will see a new determination come into your life to advance yourself and provide the best you can for your little man. you will start university as well as being a fantastic mum, you find strength you never thought you had and will learn so much in just a short time.

you will absolutely amazed to find that you slip into becoming a mum easily and that after some practise and frustration everything fits into place, into a routine and you won't ever be able to imagine your life without your little one! you will have the best year of your life!!

enjoy and cherish every moment you have with him and those around you.

love older wiser me xx

Dear Camilla,

Despite what other people may think, you are determined that being pregnant as a teen is not going to stop you from achieving. That's a thought you will need to cling to for the next few years. It's a thought you'll need to refer to every time you see a news article damning young mums (and it's almost always the mums, isn't it?), every time a news clip or programme portrays young mums as feckless individuals going nowhere fast and every time someone hints to you that you'll never amount to anything because you had a baby too young. You'll soon grow tired of these assumptions but you will keep on fighting back, you will keep on achieving and you will keep striving for more for you and your baby because that is who you are. Every step you take is not just a step for you, it's a giant leap for your baby too and it'll inspire a new way of thinking about teen mums for other people.

Being a teen mum will not be easy for you. There will be times when you are sad that your pram isn't as smart as other mum's, that you don't have a car to get around in and that you can't afford all the material things that other mums can. However, they are just that, material things. You know you will spend the first few years of your baby's life being utterly broke but you know that won't be forever as you are working towards a better life for the two of you. The things you can offer your baby are time, love, pride and a sense of ambition, all of which are free.

You're already planning on continuing on to university with your baby son. You know it'll be tiring, you'll miss out on student life and you'll frequently wonder whether working so hard is worth it. It is! Getting an education only takes a few years and you'll open up so many opportunities for yourself. You may not know anyone else who has done it, but you know that you can do it. And maybe if you succeed, another teen mum will too. Don't be afraid, you only have to take one day at a time and each day gets you that bit closer to your goals.

People may think your life has ended before it's even begun because you're pregnant. You know though that it's just taken a different course. You'll grow up faster and you'll always have someone else to consider in every choice that you make. You may have made a mistake, but as it's turned out, it's probably the best mistake you've ever made because you've never been more focused than now.

Being a pregnant teenager is not forever, but your love for your son will be.

Camilla

Camilla Chafer had her son Max when she was 18. A year later, they moved to Leeds University where Camilla gained a BA Hons in European Union Studies and a MA in European Politics (Security and Defence Analysis). She is now a freelance journalist and author.

You've come along way you know Char, you really have.

I sat down wondering, 'Shall I call the doctors yet or not?' what if I am? Nar I can't be, but what if????? The lady on the other end of the phone seemed to take forever to return with the results. Then suddenly, this loud cockney voice said 'yea luv, it's come out positive!!!!!!' I sat back in my chair in shock. Wow char, could this really be?........ 'I'm pregnant!' I felt a sense of fearful- joy come over me for a few minutes,...... then I just burst out into tears. I only turned 16 three months ago, and now........... for the rest of my life, all I'll ever be is a ....SINGLE MOTHER!!!!

I remember thinking 'Well! At least my baby will love me! After all, no one else did!!!!'................................... But I was wrong! Now I realise it wasn't a baby I needed, it was hope, ambition and stability.

When I looked down at my stomach, I could hardly believe that there was a real human life growing inside of me. It seems so surreal. I didn't even know if I can do this parenting thing! But I knew I was willing to give it my all. I thought my baby would never grow up feeling how I felt. I was gonna love him and we were gonna prove everyone wrong!....... But what happened char?......... It only took 7 months and I found myself sitting in that same spot hearing those same words!!!....... YEP, PREGNANT AGAIN!

This time things were completely different. I was slowly turning into that person I was trying so hard to prove to everyone that I wouldn't become! (Just a single mother living in a council flat and on benefits). I was a bit more mature by then but my mind was still really messed up. 'Man, what I would give to know then what I know now!'; I didn't learn though. My life was heading round a vicious cycle. 'I thought it was too late for me, a normal life that is', 20 years old 3 children and no education!!! Life just looked so bleak!!!

Looking back on things now, I don't know how I got through it all, you've done alright you know Char, things have worked out alright after all. Who would have thought, me a Christian! I've got focus now, I'm mentally and emotionally stable and I've got ambition for my life but most of all I've got hope for my future!!! Yeah I'm still a single mother, but I'm a responsible single mother, and I'm bringing up my children to know that true fulfilment can never be found without but it lies within! Now at the age of 27 my children are 10, 9 and 6 years old and I wouldn't change them for the world. There's always light at the end of the tunnel, you just have to keep heading towards it until you get there!......... The story continues.

You're sincerely

Charlene.

Dear Me,

How I wish I were 14 again, not a care in the world except who is snogging who and whether my mum will find out that I sneaked out to a club without telling her! How quickly life changes! At 16 you will meet a lovely bloke and fall head over heels in love, the perfect couple people will say! Life goes great for a while and then.........BAM! Your world will come crashing down around your ears. You split up after a silly argument and then 2 weeks later you realise that you are pregnant! He wants nothing to do with the baby and even denies that it's his! Mum goes mental and Dad just wont speak to you. It's a right old mess. All because you forget about being on the pill after taking some antibiotics for an ear infection! How my life would have been different if I had only thought!

No more clubbing, no more going away on holiday with my mates and savings......what are they?!!?

Sam, my 1st baby was born when I was 18, boy was he hard work! He had colic, hated to be left on his own and cost me a small fortune! I think that in the first year of his life I must have spent something like £4000 on nappies, clothes and toys etc! What I could have done with all that money if only I had been more careful!

I don't regret having my children one little bit but looking back I would have preferred to wait until I was a little bit older. There were so many things that I wanted to do, places I wanted to go and things I wanted to see. Now I will have to wait until the children are older. I often got very jealous of my friends when Sam was born, I was stuck in home covered in baby sick and piled high with dirty nappies and clothes to wash whilst they were out partying and having the time of their life!

Still, I had something that they didn't, my little boy. He used to look at me with his big brown eyes and all my troubles would seem so trivial. When he lay cooing to himself in his cot all I could do was smile. I am so proud of all my children and the things that they have taught me. I may have been a teenage mum but I am a great mum.

I now have 4 beautiful children, Hannah was born just 13 months after Sam, again a stupid accident, the condom split! Dom was born 3 years later and Bailey 4 years after that. Now at almost 30 I have an 11 year old, a 10 year old, a 7 year old and a 3 year old. Being a single parent was tough but I now have a wonderful husband and a great family. I have been sterilised as I really don't want any more children and I can't afford to have another accident happen!

Please think carefully about the route that you want to take in life. Babies are cute but they cost a fortune and wreck any plans that you have for the future. The pill does not work if you have sickness and diarrhoea or if you are on antibiotics. Please be careful!

You are a strong person and can do whatever you want in life, regardless of what people may think. People often think of teenage parents as selfish people who neglect their children so that they can go out partying or that they only have children to claim benefits and get a council house, I have proved them wrong, yes I may still live in a council house but we work hard for everything we have and I can't remember the last time I went out on my own!

Have a great life

Clair

Dear me,

Hindsight what a fabulous thing, if only I knew what I know now when I first became a mum at 17 hey!!! I remember you plodding along, worrying about being the best mum in the world, hating all the advice that kept coming from the so called OLDER BETTER PARENTS. Who did they think they were?? Well now girl, I am that older mum, maybe better, maybe not, but I got here and my boy grew up to be a fantastic man. I did good. Do you remember those times when all our friends were going out and having fun, going on holiday together??? Remember how one minute everyone was there to see the lovely baby, cooing over him, THEN suddenly they'd gone. Where were all these friends that would be there to support me??? Where were my list of for-life babysitters???? It was hard kiddo wasn't it, BUT it's worth it now. We struggled along and felt useless at times, but now I am offering all those "Friends" some of the wisdom I have gained through being a parent. All the times people would say to me "don't do that" " Do it this way" Well now they are saying sorry to me because they realise that even though they're older than what I was it doesn't always work that way and we can only do our best.

If I could turn the clocks back there isn't much I'd do differently, EXCEPT.... ACCEPT a little more help from the "OLDER MORE EXPERIENCED MUMS AND DADS"", AND I'd ask for help instead of trying to do everything by myself.

We made mistakes BUT WE also did a good job.   Don't sit and struggle, ASK if you need help or SUPPORT. TALK if you want to.   ENJOY bringing the child up, because the time goes so quick. I'm 39 now and whilst all my friends are just starting their journey, I now help younger parents with their journey and am starting one of my own. The holidays have started and I'm actually old enough to enjoy it.

LIFE DIDN'T STOP WHEN WE HAD OUR SON, THE JOURNEY BEGAN.

Dear Carolyn,

I know it's scary getting pregnant at 15, and I know it feels like everyone is judging you. I want you to know that it's going to be OK.

When you got pregnant you were out of control, you had no respect for anyone not even yourself. But having a baby is a really positive thing for you. It's going to help you get straight, because you have to think about someone else. You made a choice to keep it and Vince stood by you — he always will no matter what — and you changed who you are for the better.

You become a really good mum, who would do anything for her kids. You manage to get out of the negative situation you are in and build a better life for yourself. No one is going to judge you badly because you were a teenage mum, in fact people only want to help you, and you need to let them help. They don't see the scared and fragile teen, they see a mature and sensible mum who has overcome so much to get want she wants.

And you can still go to university! You will have to work hard, and it's going to be tough, but you will get there, and do what you want to do, and enjoy it. It will take you longer, but that's OK, don't be so hard on yourself.

Eventually, you will get a degree and a teaching qualification, despite having 2 more children. You make it because you are stronger than you realize.

I know you are worried about what kind of a parent you will be; I know you haven't had the best experiences. But this helps you do better. You look at your kids and think, what is best for them? You will be a loving caring mum; your boys will be hard working and polite. Everyone will think they are great, because you do a good job.

Getting pregnant now may seem like a really scary big thing you can't handle, but please know that you can, and do, handle it all really well. You turn out just fine, and so do your children. You achieve what you set out to, and you enjoy it.

It all turns out well for you.

Love
The Future You
xxx

Dear David

Or perhaps I should call you Dave - everyone else did when you were nineteen, except your mother. Ann still does, as it happens. Yes, it's been forty-five years now, we're still together, and the girls are grown up. Oops! - you didn't know you were going to have a girl, did you, still less more than one of them. Don't worry, there are only two and they've turned out okay.

You're a lance-corporal in the Royal Signals, serving in Germany. The money's not great, but as a technician you're better paid than the average soldier and it's enough. Strictly speaking, your wife should be at home living with her parents - in your day soldiers weren't entitled to married accommodation until they were twenty-one, but you've managed with a succession of locally rented rooms and married quarters borrowed while the occupants were away on long courses.

So, from your own distant future I suppose I should be offering you sage advice about impending parenthood and helping you to avoid pitfalls. Trouble is, so far as I can remember, you didn't actually do much wrong. Having a baby quite so soon probably wasn't a brilliant move, but then it wasn't planned and it worked out pretty well in the end anyway. In years to come you'll be the envy of friends who daren't let their toddlers near the swimming pool, while your girls are old enough and sensible enough to go and swim on their own. Later on, they'll be in demand for baby sitting.

34

The baby's due in September, by which time you'll be twenty. And she'll be early - more on that later. I probably shouldn't have told you that it's a she: these days we have scans and things that would seem like science fiction to you back in 1965; people know what sex their children are going to be well before the event, if they want to, and they know whether there's likely to be anything wrong with them, too. In your day you just trusted nature to take its course and found out what you'd got when it arrived.

Which brings me to something you have wondered about. All prospective parents wonder whether their babies are going to be all right. In one way, you and Ann are probably less worried than most. She's worked with handicapped children and you've spent lots of time with them, so you don't have that awful, gnawing doubt as to whether you'd be able to cope if your baby had problems. You know you could hack it. But there's no need to worry, anyway - she'll be fine, ten fingers, ten toes and bright as a button.

And although she wasn't planned you'll love her to bits; your family is started, and the next one will be planned. Your little girl will get a baby sister when she's about two.

So what can I tell you that might make life a bit easier? Not a lot, if we're honest. One thing is always carry a door key. In August, Ann will go to the military hospital at Iserlohn for a routine check up;

they'll be a bit worried about her blood pressure and they'll keep her in. You'll get home, realise you haven't got a key, and you'll shin up the drainpipe at the back of the house and squeeze in through the open fanlight in the bathroom. It's not a recommended method of entry.

Another thing: make sure you've always got a full packet of fags. I don't smoke, but you do. You'll go along to visit your wife in hospital one day at the end of August and find her bed empty. The sister will tell you they've brought the baby on early and she's in the delivery ward. These days you'd scrub up and take your place at her side. No, really! In your day men weren't supposed to know that childbirth is a painful, messy business. You knew your place – sitting in a waiting room, chain smoking, until there was news, and then you'd be taken in to see the new mum, who'd been scrubbed up to look as though nothing much had happened. On that visit, you probably wouldn't even see the baby.

As it happens, you will see yours. As you're led to the delivery ward, not quite sure what to expect, a nurse will be wheeling out a trolley. She'll realise that you're the father and will introduce you to your daughter. You'll look down into the trolley and see this tiny, tiny, pink, blotchy thing and realise that it's a person, your own flesh and blood, and it's a moment that you'll remember for the rest of your life.

Oh yes, about the fags. When you discover that Ann's in labour, and you're in for a long night, you'll also realise that you've got about two cigarettes. "Dad" Walker, the (incredibly old) duty driver who brought you to the hospital doesn't smoke. You'll shoot off to the Naafi shop, which is closed. "Dad" will bang on the doors and throw stones at the staff accommodation windows until, against all the odds, a young woman opens up the shop and sells you a couple of packets of Senior Service tipped.

So there you go: carry a front door key and don't run out of cigarettes. As advice goes, it's hardly profound and certainly not life changing, but then you don't really need your life changing, do you? You're doing all right, mate. Keep it up.

All the best.

David (aged 64)

Dear Grace (aged 19. 1942)

It was so good to hear that after 22 months of marriage you're expecting your first baby and that you are over the moon about it! These times are so precarious, with Bill being away at War, and I know you wanted a baby in case anything happened to him. You aren't alone, there are a lot of girls out there who are in the same situation as you two, the future seems so uncertain at the moment. I just want you to know that he will be fine, be a great Dad and you two will be spending many, many happy years together. In fact, in a few years you'll be having your second baby together, I won't spoil the surprise of what you're having this time but you'll have one of each!

I know it can be lonely with Bill being away but you have your job in the Haberdashery shop to keep you busy plus all the things to get ready for the baby. I know you love knitting and needle work, that yellow with tiny red roses pram set you're making is beautiful!

It's great that you are enjoying the pregnancy too and knowing there is a part of Bill close with you all the time must be very comforting.

The days will soon speed by until the baby is born but don't worry, your Mum is only over the bridge if you need any help, and you'll soon get used to having a new little person around, Bill will even make it home for a short visit!

With life so uncertain and Bill away it may seem like all you can do is just get on with it but don't worry, I can tell you this, you will be a wonderful Mum!

With lots of love

Grace (aged 88. 2010)

Dear Hannah (17 years)

You have just found out you're pregnant, you are so excited and so is Matthew. Although you're not nervous you can't help but wonder what the future holds for you and your baby. Well here is an insight for you....

You will face some tough times after the birth of your baby but life is always throwing challenges at you and you just smile your way through them. Here are a few survival tips for when this happens:

* *Smile, this is the toughest weapon you have*

* *Ignore your neighbours and remember you will be in your lovely home soon*

* *Don't burn your bridges, you never know when you will need them*

* *Make lots of new friends and don't be trampled on*

* *Most importantly, remember you're a survivor*

These might sound strange now but as you go on through your life you will realise why you need them. You spend 15 months in a hostel and you hate it but it really will be worth it when you get your house and turn it into a palace for you and your daughter....yes you have a little girl! She is born on father's day (17th June 2007) at 4.27am weighing 8lb 2oz. She is gorgeous.

She is beautiful, she has blonde hair now and the biggest blue eyes you can imagine! She makes you laugh every single day and it hurts your heart you love her that much. You face a particular tough time in the summer of 2009 when you get diagnosed with cervical cancer. Don't panic! You can get through this you know you can, you only have to look at Jayleigh Kate to know what you have to live for. She is your world and she idolises you. Her smile gets you through everything else and this is no different.

Despite the obvious bad things, you have also achieved a lot since Jayleigh was born...

* Passed your driving test and got your own car

* Got your own home

* Learnt to cook

* Became a youth worker and you love it

* Worked the summer in a bar and met nice friends

* Finished your first year at college and you're on your second

* You're planning on going to university to become a Health Promotion Specialist

* Kept up good relationships with your friends and family, this includes Matthew

* Taken Jayleigh on many girls only trips to the seaside and came home in one piece

* Did a skydive from 12,500ft and lived to tell the tale

* Most importantly, you have survived cancer!

Hopefully your survival guide will come in useful over many more years and you can then pass it onto Jayleigh. You are an inspirational young woman Hannah, not only to yourself and Jayleigh but to others around you. Keep up the good work!

Hannah (20 years)

Dear Jade,

I am writing you this letter to let you know you do not need to be worried about your future, I know you are 18 now and pregnant with your first child but your life does not need to stop . You are 27 now and have come a long way, you will be moving into your first home soon, I know it is not going to be yours but you will not be renting a house forever. In 18 months you will buy your own house, one that you can make your own and decorate how you want it! You will carry on working for the government when you have finished your maternity leave and will also get a promotion and get recognized for your skills.

You will meet a lot of good friends along the way, through your children (yes you will have more!)and the groups you will join when you have your baby, it will be hard work and you will have a lot of responsibility but it will make you stronger as a person, a very good friend once said to me 'women are like tea bags, you don't realise how strong you are until you are in hot water' and it's very true.

You will manage looking after your baby and working to live your life to the full, you will achieve the things you always wanted to and even jump out of a plane!

You will get married in a couple of years, and also pass your driving test in the same year! You will pass an NVQ through your work and also go on to do courses in IT and floristry, where you will hopefully start your own business one day. You just need to remember to follow your dreams and keep believing that anything is possible with hard work and determination. Like I said it won't be easy and there will be a lot of hard days but things will always get better. Even the hard days will do you good and make you ready for the next challenge, everything in life happens for a reason and makes you a better person in the long run.

When you do have your second child, you will discover more and more opportunities in your area, with sure start centres and different groups for young mums. When your children start school you will get to watch them develop into individuals and be able to help them achieve their goals as well as your own, and there is no better repayment for all your hard work than when your children give you a hug and tell you they love you. You will be able to be proud of them and what they achieve and you should be proud of yourself for everything you have done so far.

Now you just need to try and remember to make time for yourself, and not to feel guilty about the things you don't always get round to doing (normally the ironing!) you will always get there in the end!

Good luck for the future, always reach for your dreams...

Jade

Dear Maria,

I know you're really worried right now. The nurse at the university health centre has just told you that you are pregnant, and when you began to cry she snapped, 'Did you think it wouldn't happen to you?' And I suppose you didn't think it would happen to you; after all you had been taking the pill but not always at the same time each day, in truth you'd missed a few, taken a few, and then went to get the morning after pill. The morning after pill didn't work, it has a failure rate and you were one of the few girls that fell into that small band. The response you were about to get wasn't good: the doctor said, 'No problem, we can arrange for you to have a termination between lectures, you needn't miss any studies.' It wasn't even a choice for you — you knew you were going to have a baby and carry on with your studies, you knew you were strong, what you didn't yet know was how difficult life was going to become.

Pretty soon it became apparent that you were on your own in this; the response from the father was poor. Throughout the pregnancy you tried to involve him but he was insulting and difficult. Your mother was with you when your son was born and you held him in your arms thinking that having a baby was the most beautiful experience ever and you must do it again sometime. He was gorgeous. Giving birth had been painful, but wondrous too – two weeks later you enrolled on a college course to study sociology A-level and breastfed him as you wrote your essays. Lessons took place one evening a week, studying kept your motivation going.

You went to the Jobcentre to ask about going back to part-time work and returning to university; the lone parent advisor did the sums and told you that it wasn't possible. You left the appointment with the intention of proving her wrong. Everything is possible, you told yourself, all you need is a way and the motivation. You contacted a tutor at the University of Manchester and he agreed for you to complete a degree in 3 years rather than 4, and instead of a year in Spain, you can study in Spain for three months at a language course; you'll take your son with you. You also found a number of part-time jobs, you graduated and then went on to take an MA – it was then everything improved and you met a wonderful group of friends and work colleagues.

It didn't work out well with your son's father, he was abusive and for quite some years you were petrified of him. What I want to tell you is that there are going to be some very tough years ahead, and sometimes you think that you'll never rise above being perpetually broke and feeling depressed because you are living in a cold council house and life is just horrible. There will be times when life seems to be work and tears, but it passes — ten years on you will move to London, share a household with other single parents and have fulfilled your dream of being a writer.

For a long time you felt ashamed of being a single mother, like you had somehow failed. You found it hard to talk with other mums but after a while it became easier. Now your son is 11 and you are in your early thirties. Throughout this time your son has been a wonder, he began to talk very early on and since that day he has made you laugh. He is kind and considerate, witty, smart, everything to you and you love him dearly. The truth is, that if you hadn't fallen pregnant with your son at 19, you would not be the person you are today.

Do not worry, do not cry — there are some really good times ahead, you'll fall in love and out of love and generally life is fun. Your son is a special gift to you, and you're going to be a kind and loving mum.

So, come on... don't listen to that nurse, wipe your eyes and stride out of there — you've got a life to be lived and it's going to be so very full. I'd recommend having a quick nap, you're going to need all the energy you have. But it's not a problem, the great thing is you're young, you have the energy, and plenty of time ahead of you too. Women get pregnant, you are female, don't be crushed by what is happening to your body and those idiots who make you feel down — good luck sweetheart, but I know you don't need it, everything is going turn out just fine.... better than fine.

Maria Roberts
Author of Single Mother on the Verge (Penguin)

Dear Sarah

I know that you're struggling at the moment, constantly arguing with your parents and moving from one parent to the other before finally settling at your dads.

Your next birthday you're going to meet a man who at first you think is the best thing in your life until you realize you're being controlled and manipulated, as a couple of years go on you will stick at the relationship trying to make things work. Not long after your 16th birthday you will find out you're pregnant with a little girl you will soon realise that you have to get yourself and daughter away from this man and start afresh, you will then find a place for you and your little girl to live where you can both be safe and happy together. You will then go on to University where you will study counselling and hopefully graduate as a fully trained counsellor and will be able to provide properly for you and your daughter.

Chin up girl
Love Sarah (age 20)

Dear Trish (aged 18)

Oh my gosh you are pregnant. You are so so happy as being a mother is all you have ever wanted to be. Having a little person you can love and cherish and who will love you back unconditionally is all that matters. You have a lovely mum and dad but because of your weight issues and bullying you have always yearned to be accepted and not judged by anyone. You are smitten with your boyfriend who is 7 years your senior and he has been through it all before so will be there to help you through it all (or so you think). Just one thing is playing on your mind; how will I tell my parents? Well you will move out of home and in with David before you do, you know you always look for no fuss option. Also that way no one can stop you starting your little family. It will all be new and exciting but at the same time scary. You will feel you have let down some of your family as you see the look of disappointment on their faces when you tell them you are going to be a teen mum with not the most desirable man in the village being the father. Well all that will pass because they love you and just as they have loved and supported you as a child they will see little Chloe when she is born and immediately fall in love with her as you did from the first time you felt her move in your tummy. Here are some other little tips I think might put your mind at rest as time goes by:

- Don't be too impatient for the birth, enjoy every minute of every day with her no matter how difficult. She will grow so quickly you will wish you could slow down time. Take as many pictures as you can she will blossom and grow and but your eyes and memory won't keep pace.

- There is no such thing as a perfect mum so be your own person and don't take to heart what other people say. You know your baby best and you will do anything to make her safe, loved and happy.

- Don't be scared to ask for help, if you are tired and feeling washed out it's not a sign of weakness it is NORMAL. Babies are lovely but very tiring. Your big sister who frowned at first will become like a second mum and adore her as much as you do.

- Being hit by your partner is not your fault and you don't deserve it. Please walk away with your head held high. Don't be frightened of the temporary accommodation the council put you in. It is safe for you and Chloe and you will have six interesting months there before getting your own house which you will make into the home you still live in now.

- Don't think just because you are a mum now your role in life will always be to care for people and put yourself second. You will become confident and make decisions about your future that you want to make and which are right for you and your family. (try to make them earlier, you can do it if you put your mind to it!!)

- You left school with no qualifications but once you have put your mind to it you will get yourself back to college at the age of 23 and move successfully from college into a job you will then lead to University and you will fulfil an ambition you never thought possible. On graduation day your mum and sister will be by your side and the pride will shine on all your faces.

- You married David at 20 years old because it is the done thing, domestic violence saw you split up for 12 months just a year later. The marriage will last until you are 29 and then you will be a single mum again, don't worry you are now older, wiser and stronger and you will cope very well.

- You will work hard and balance looking after by now both Chloe and Harry and a wonderful job. You are a good role model to your children.

- Don't feel guilty for not being at every school event you will realise its quality not always quantity of time you spend with your children as time goes by. The kids will love the time you spend with them when you get home and the lovely holidays you get to take them on.

This letter doesn't cover everything and won't answer half of the questions you have going through your head but hopefully it will put you at ease to know that no matter how hard it feels at times, things will turn out fine and you will feel like the luckiest lady on earth in years to come and grateful for all the experience you have gained in life. Chloe will be a beautiful 18 years old in September 2010 and the age you were when you became pregnant; you made it full circle mum.xx

Lots of love
Trish (aged 37)

Ellie, Steve's Wife

Being a young mum doesn't mean you are irresponsible, it just means you are lucky enough to experience parenthood at a young age. What I can say is life is a roller coaster, just go with the flow and don't let it take you over. Your children look to you for guidance so tell them you love them every day, greet them with a smile, encourage their dreams and aspirations, allow them to be themselves and not what YOU want them to be.

I wish you all that you wish for yourselves.

Ellie XX

Steve, Ellie's Husband

Young Mums are usually plagued by that frustrating phenomenon called "young Fathers". New Mums suddenly find themselves caring for not one, but two, helpless, demanding, time consuming and often selfish individuals. Faced with the fact that they now find themselves taking second place, and having to become a 'responsible' adult who is expected to share and often take charge of the newborns daily routine, the young Father becomes 'confused young Father'.

Feeding, changing, bathing are not life skills he inherited from the 'lads at football/down the gym'. Give him time to come to terms with the monumental shift in the balance of power. Like the baby, he will learn from your lead. it might take time and a few tantrums (easy on the door slamming), but eventually he can be moulded into 'proud young Dad'. be strong, compassionate and caring towards him. But most importantly, always be RIGHT!

Steve (an old dad)

Dear You,

I know you are all over the place in your head at the moment but take a breath, step back and try to see what you are doing. Please don't give up going to school. You will regret it for ever.

You are right, it is massively exciting to be growing a tiny person inside you but it is also the scariest thing you will ever do. You are about to need to grow up and that means thinking about the future. You cannot rely on anyone but yourself and the sooner you realise that the better you will feel.

There is going to be so much joy to come, the embarrassment you feel at being pregnant will be overcome by the tiny being you will bring into the world.

Put her first. Always. Before anyone else, including yourself.

You are going to go through loads of bad stuff and it will feel like you are broken but you are not broken and you are worthy and you will come out of it a stronger person.

Enjoy parenting, count to a million throughout all the screaming, trust your instincts - they are usually right, and be happy.

Love Me.

So, 2 weeks after your 18th birthday, and you think you're pregnant. But, you're too scared to go out and buy a pregnancy test — what if someone you know sees you? What if the old woman who works in the supermarket tells your Mum? What if, what if, what if. All that runs through your mind is what if. It's constant, like a train going nowhere. You don't have any answers. You're scared. You want to tell your Mum, you want her to comfort you, and tell you everything is going to be OK. But you just can't. You follow her round aimlessly for a few days, trying to just spit the words out, but they don't come.

For me? Eventually, she figured it out herself. My Mum, 8 weeks later, came into my bedroom and just spat it out — 'are you pregnant?'. I burst into tears. She held me. We chat, for the longest time. She is supportive no matter what my decision, but tells me she cannot be at the birth with me, because I am her daughter, and she can't watch me go through that.

I'm 23 now, very nearly 24. I have three children. If I could talk to myself 5 years ago, what would I say? I'd be truthful. You are about to go through one of the hardest things you'll ever do. You'll face prejudice, stereotypes, and hardship. Every mother does, for one reason or another. But, your age will be against you at the moment of conception. Some people will sympathise, some will think you're in it for the money and a council house. Without a doubt, they will assume your baby is an accident, and you're no longer as a couple. Whatever. It hurts, and at times you feel ashamed. But, you know what? You are just as capable of being a great parent as someone 20 years older. You aren't wasting your life, you aren't doomed to a life of benefits and council housing. No matter how bleak things seem, you have the most wonderful incentive to do well in life — your child.

Hold your head high, always. Never let anyone put you down, and never let your age be a barrier to anything you want to do. For every person that looks down on you, there will be another who admires you for the fantastic job you do in the face of hardship. You can do it, and you can do it well.

Emily, Mummy to Aiden — 5, William — 2.5, and Jessica — 1.

Dear 16 year old me,

I know you're pregnant and I know you're scared, I also know you're extremely excited at what lies ahead! You should be, parenthood is all you expected and more, of course you at the time believed love was forever and J's dad would always be there for you and for him no matter what. Never fear, I know initially it will be a rough ride and you will find things tough and at times you will wonder how you are going to survive in the world, alone with a son. But you do and two years down the track you are coping marvellously and loving every second.

You've learnt to respect yourself and that you dont need someone else to make you complete and to love you, you can do that all by yourself. You've learnt to love your body, your c-section scar and that mummy tum because they are all part of you. You've even excepted your uniqueness of having two uteri and now are proud of it rather than ashamed, mainly with the help of your gynaecologist.

J's birth left deep scars and did lead to Post Natal Depression but you conquered that and are now an amazing parent. Don't worry so much about everything you do, you will soon realise that the most important thing to your little man is that you are there for him, that's the most important thing to him!

You are going to appreciate your female friends a lot more and turn your back a great deal on the many male friends you had early teens. The close friendship you will find through retaking your maths GCSE at evening school will turn into your best friend and surrogate sister. You will be joined at the hip and experience many highs and lows together.

Prior to having J you struggled with your grandparents death but once you have that little man and you take him to your grandparents house for the last time before it is sold you will feel more at peace. You also take him with you when you go to visit the places we scattered their ashes and that little person gives you your strength.

You may not believe it but you will turn into a fine young lady and a wonderful mother, you are fun, outgoing, confident and happy, all while being single, which I know at the moment at 16 you don't believe is possible because you can only see the nuclear family of two parents and child but you will live alone, you will be happy doing so and one day you will find happiness with someone who compliments you rather than completes you.

Believe in yourself Hayley because you can do it and you will :)

Hayley

Dear My Pregnant Self (age 16)

I don't know whether you know you're pregnant yet. If you don't, get a test done. It will be positive. But I think you already know that really.

I know that everything just feels really scary right now. People at college are gonna look at you like you're a freak for a few months. You will get a lot of 'pity' looks too which, strangely enough, doesn't make you feel any better. I know it's hard to be positive about how things will turn out but, I promise, the second that baby is born you will fall head over heels in love and suddenly it really won't matter what anyone else thinks.

Not everyone has decided that your life is over though. With invaluable help from Grandma and Grandad (previously known as Mum and Dad) and a supportive college tutor you are able to continue your A levels and get a degree. This then enables you to get a good job, buy a house, do a Masters and go on some much more exciting holidays than the ones you were dragged on a child. It won't stop people looking at you in disbelief and saying you can't possibly be old enough to have a child of that age. But you learn to take it as a compliment rather than an insult, whether it was meant as one or not. People may say you did everything the wrong way round but you will never consider that you did because you wont be able to imagine not having your son to share all your favourite moments with.

Time goes so quickly so have fun and enjoy being a Mum - it's the most important job you will ever do. But then, I think you already know that too.

Joelle (age 30)
x

P.S. Even though you are young you will still never be considered 'cool' in the eyes of your son. To him, you are just the same as every other embarrassing Mum!

P.P.S. Follow your instincts. They are pretty much always right!

Dear Kathryn

I don't think that anyone truly realises how much motherhood will change them until it happens. We assume we can fit a baby into our existing lifestyle, what we don't realise is how we have to change our lives to incorporate a new arrival.

You were 19 when you fell pregnant with your beautiful daughter. The pregnancy wasn't planned and it didn't take too long to realise that you would be bringing her up on your own. I think you always imagine the perfect scenario when you dream of what it will be like when you eventually start a family. The house, the husband, the 2.4 children, and not only did you have to cope with the prospect of having a child on your own, the 'dream situation' was also shattered and this was also just as hard to deal with.

Your life changed the moment you found out that you were pregnant, the non stop social whirl you so enjoyed came abruptly to a halt, the packet of cigarettes in your coat pocket went straight into the bin and alcohol wouldn't pass your lips for some years to come. Severe morning sickness forced you to change your working hours to ensure you weren't late for work every day and you became a social leper, suddenly no longer of interest to many of your so called friends.

And then it happened, you started bleeding. On a visit to the hospital's early pregnancy unit for a scan to check if you had miscarried, you were informed you had lost your baby, but it's twin was still thriving! At just 6 weeks, the little peanut shaped blob on the screen was the most beautiful thing you had ever seen and you became fiercely protective of the little 'peanut' that eventually became your daughter. Losing your daughter's twin made you realise that although you were young and on your own, you wanted the baby more than you wanted anything else.

By the time your daughter was born in January 2002, you were, you thought, ready to be a mum. What a shock you were in for! The sleepless nights, constant feeding and nappy changing, no time for yourself, moving into your own home when your daughter was 2 months old and feeling more alone than you have ever felt in your life.

It took just one thing to alter the state of depression that you found yourself in. Four years ago you started working part time. You wanted to be there for your daughter and be able to take her to and from her new school, which you wouldn't have been able to do if you had continued to work full time. You had missed out on so much of your daughter by working so much and wanted to be what you considered a 'real' mum. The post natal depression you suffered from affected your choice of job, supporting people with mental health problems, some of whom had post natal depression just like you did. This eventually expanded to included people with drug and alcohol dependency, ex offenders, vulnerable families and young mums, which you particularly enjoy. It has given you the opportunity to use your experience of being a young mum and having post natal depression to help others.

If you had not had your daughter you would not have chosen the profession you are in. She has made you more aware of the problems faced by other people, far more responsible and empathetic and has given you a different kind of confidence in yourself and your abilities. If you want something you don't just wait for it to fall into your lap, you go out and get it for yourself, no matter how much hard work it takes.

You will have your fair share of ups and downs once you become a mother and at times things will be difficult, but your daughter will change your life for the better and you will like the person she makes you become!

Love

Me x

Finding Out!

So you did a test as a joke with your friend and it backfired by being positive! Well don't panic, it will be the making of you.

Don't ignore this because it won't go away as much as you would like it to. So the father had walked away and doesn't want to know, it's ok you will do a great job on your own. Your child will turn out to be a confident, happy typical teenager.

7 months gone and you've finally told your parents. Wasn't so hard really. As for your mum telling you she's disappointed in you, that disappointment will become pride, because you will be a great mum

After birth

Don't panic about the feelings you're having. Despite everyone telling you about this rush of love you will feel when you first see your baby, the numb feeling is OK a lot of women feel it too. You do love your baby and you will feel it soon. It doesn't make you a freak or a terrible person because you feel nothing but emptiness. It will happen in time and you feel love for your daughter. So much so that you will realize you want to make a career for yourself and your daughter.

You must enjoy having a baby instead of worrying about what other people will say or whether they will judge you.

Your bills are important and need to be paid.

You will have a 2nd child who will be loved as much as your first, the father will stick by you and be a great help. He too will love your daughter as his own.

Your daughter's biological father has missed out and you can take full credit for raising your daughter and despite her teenage tantrums, you will be proud of her. Be proud of yourself too!

Dear Jenny

The hardest thing for you all those years ago was telling your parents you were pregnant and feeling that your pregnancy would destroy their lives, so you didn't say anything. You took what you saw was your only option and ran away with your baby's father after finishing your A Levels, keeping your pregnancy a secret. You knew that you would have to work and study even harder to prove to yourself and your family that you could be a young parent and have a career.

One of the nicest presents, a week or so after your daughter was born, were the hand knitted baby clothes from your gran and later that first summer your Gran and Grandad came to stay and visit their first great grandchild.

Moving around and sharing houses with different people, with not a lot of money didn't stop you and your daughter from making the most of opportunities that came your way.

You certainly don't have any regrets, you have a lovely happy bright daughter and 2 fantastic grandsons. You learnt so much as you both helped each other.

You enjoy your work and you are sure that being a young parent shaped your career in youth and community work, where you have delivered and developed services that empower and enable other people and strive for justice and equality. You have been active as a volunteer in children's and youth work and now you assist organisations at a strategic level, writing bids, on Boards and as a leader and manager. You enjoy holidays, walking and music.

Throughout your life you have invested in your daughter and her education and future and know that her parents, friends, aunts, uncles, grandparents and extended family treasure her and value her for who she is — a strong woman, a loving parent and wife with a career and family she adores.

Dear Pregnant Lianne

Hey girl!

Well... What a long way we have come, yet still as ditzy! I will tell you from now, the coco butter did not work you still ended up getting stretch marks and no, your stomach will never be the same again!! But you do have a beautiful cheeky bright lil princess, so you don't have to spend £75 on a private scan to find out if it's a girl, just so you can call her Destiny!

You don't have to stress as much as you are! Your dad will start speaking to you again; he just needs time to get to grips with the fact that he is going to be a granddad! He loves Destiny more than ever now she is here!!

How you're feeling will not last forever your head is all over the place because this is not what you planned for yourself, but believe me things will start to look up! Being depressed does not help anything look in the mirror and bring back that friendly, outgoing loving h.o.t.t. girl we all love! You have not given up despite your ups and downs and have lost some special people in your life along the way. Please remember to take Destiny to see Leroy, Aunty Babs and her great granddad as they are looking down from up above now.

You do not need to be in a rush to find your own place although you and mum are not getting along at the

68

moment she does chill out and you two actually have quite a good relationship now! It's kinda scary you always said you will never do things like her, but oh you do!!! When it comes to you and you know who.. It's not a happy ending I'm afraid, there's still potential there but you have to learn to compromise and treat him with a little more respect and let your guard down! Not all men are the same so stop using the past as an excuse to mess up your future girl!!

You will never guess what you're doing now!?! You are an adviser in Connexions! You always said you wanted to work with young people but didn't think you could do it once you became pregnant, because you didn't finish college. Well you did girl and this is only the beginning. You're actually advising young parents, so although working for USC was cool we knew that's where we didn't want to end up!

It's about time I wrap this up, you know me I can write for ever. By the way don't give up writing your poems and plays, it helps you to relax and you love it. Make time to do that if anything! And don't stop your driving lessons cause you still can't drive now!! (I told you I can go on and on). Right back to wrapping it up... I am proud of you, you went from a young pregnant girl to a yummy mummy not only that but a woman, a phenomenal woman. Not to beep my own horn.. actually what the heck BEEP BEEP!!!
Love you lots
An older still ditzy Lianne
Xxx

To Lucy,

You will have a very rough four years ahead of you, but it will make you stronger. You will have two gorgeous children that love and adore you. Remember your mum loves you and she does what she can, so remember to thank her. Talk to your mum and Gemma, they will help you even when you think no one can help you. Stay strong and enjoy the time you have with your special babies, they are both amazing. Don't stress yourself out too much, everything happens for a reason and you will come to realise that in time. just remember don't trust everyone, not everyone is who you think they are. Listen to your instincts because they are usually right. Please don't stay quiet when you're on the way to the church, SHOUT and say you really feel, you will know what I mean when the time comes.

all the best

  Lucy x

Dear Vicki (17)

So... you're pregnant. Not quite in line with the life plan that you had mapped out, but although it might seem scary now, things are going to work out OK.

First things first. Tell mum and dad! When they said they would throw you out if you got pregnant that was just their way of telling you that you needed to be careful. You're going to arrange to leave school, to find somewhere to live and make all sorts of practical arrangements before you pluck up the courage to tell them. News flash! You've been acting so weirdly that they've guessed that something isn't right and they're imagining all sorts of things. So, put them out of their misery! You have no idea of this now, but they are on your side and their love and support are going to keep you going through some really tough times ahead of you. It's only when you become a mum yourself that you'll realise how much they love you and want to protect you.

There are so many life lessons that you're going to learn over the years, but there are a few things that I would love for you to know now, so that at least some of them might be a little easier.

Enjoy being pregnant and don't hide away. You're going to get so used to blending into the background so that you don't stand out. But this is a time that is so precious and it's irreplaceable. You have a little boy growing inside you who is going to be the centre of your world and give you a reason for being. People are always quick to judge and to disapprove but you need to learn not to take everything to heart. You'll waste so much time over the years worrying what people think when what really matters is the people that you love.

Being a young parent can be a tough call. And you're going to be on your own with Josh for a long time. Once the thought of the responsibility of becoming a parent hits home to his dad you won't see him for dust. So, double whammy. Single teenage parent. You will find that this gives people licence to feel that it's OK to comment on every aspect of your life, to think that you're fair game. Get used to it because it's going to last a very long time. However, you will draw strength from their disapproval and it will spur you on to make sure that nothing will stand in your way to achieve what you set out to.

Your life isn't over. You're just not going to have the life you expected to. You're going to learn to fight for what you want and to become stronger than you ever thought possible. You have no idea how much being a mum will transform your dreams and expectations and how much drive you will develop to make sure that Josh never goes without.

Back to your quest to be invisible... You will shy away from mums and toddlers groups because you feel that people will look down on you and when Josh gets a bit older you'll scurry through the school gates at the last minute so that you don't have to feel the stares of the cliques of middle class parents boring through you. Stand tall and proud.

You are a good mum and you are working hard to ensure a safe and secure life for your family of two. You'll learn as you get older that most people's outer confidence covers a mass of insecurities and that age isn't an indicator of the ability to parent. Believe me, when you get older and the 'you don't look old enough' comments start to fade, you'll miss them!

Although you think your education is over, your head teacher will be one of the inspirational women that helps you to believe that anything is possible. She will fight for your corner to make sure you can stay in school to take your exams and will be an incredible advocate in the months to come. She will be one of a few people in your life who believe in you, even when your faith in yourself is wavering. Treasure these people and embrace their help. It's OK to accept support - it's not a sign of weakness but one of strength. It will take you a long time to realise this.

You're going to sit your exams six weeks after you've given birth. You'll be sleep deprived and feel like your brain is mush but you're going to pass all of them with good enough grades to get your University place. Your newly revived resolve is going to inspire you to retake the one that you don't feel you've done well enough in and you're going to pass it with flying colours. You're going to go to University and although it isn't quite what you're expecting and you'll wish many times that you'd chosen a different path, you're going to get through it and it's going to give you the foundation for a good career.

Never be ashamed of being a young parent. What have you got to apologise for? And being a working parent isn't a weakness - you'll be surrounded by them! You'll be so concerned that people will think it will reflect badly on you that one time you'll work for someone for more than six months before they have any idea that you have a son. Again with the invisibility...

Your son will always know that he is loved and that he is number one in your life. He will have the love and support of an incredible aunty and grandparents. You're never going to be a perfect mother or a perfect person but you'll find that perfection doesn't exist in people. You'll do the best that you can and it won't be all that bad!

Finally, please try to learn to trust people and to accept advice (at least some of it, even with a truckload of salt), with good grace. I know that you won't want to listen to me because you are probably the most stubborn person that I have ever known, but if you know best - and this letter's from you - it's going to take some going even for you to kick against it.

Cherish every moment,

Vicki (37)

Dear Marie

I am looking back on you from 34 year old woman I now am, and I see how naive you are at 17 years old, becoming a single parent. Initially you will think life will be easy but over the years you will struggle emotionally and financially trying to raise a son alone with no support.

Looking back I feel so proud, not only of the level headed, respectful man that my son has become, but how I have struggled through adversity to make a success of my life. My advice to you would be to always make time for yourself, your son means everything to you, but carve out a career for yourself, because as your child grows up, and eventually leaves home, you will find yourself with no life of your own if you do not pursue some time for yourself and your interests. It is very hard to get to know yourself and who you are, when you go straight from being a child, to caring for one, so consider your own future carefully as well as your sons.

In the early years, do not make any stupid choices regarding boyfriends. You don't need support from a man enough to put up with being mistreated, you are much stronger than you think. Your choices do not just affect you anymore. There are two kinds of people in life, you can either be a soldier or a victim - you are a soldier - in time you will see what I mean.

You left school well before you should have, with no qualifications, but you will get back into education, learn to drive and have a good career and have an immense sense of pride that you have done all this alone while raising your son with no help from anyone.

When you get to my age it seems that time has passed by very quickly, although it does not seem like it at the time when times are hard – but it truly does go fast so enjoy your son! Enjoy when he is young and take more photos!

Give the baby a kiss from me

Love Marie x

Dear Petra, age 19.

I know how upset and terrified you are at the idea of being pregnant, giving birth and by being a parent and I know that you feel like you have disappointed people and let everybody down, but you haven't. When your Mum asks you "what are you crying for, this is a joyous occasion not a sad one", she'll be right you know! Your Baby will be the best thing that has ever happened to you although it doesn't seem like that it at this moment in time. Your Son will be your very own Ray of Sunshine that will give you a purpose and the drive to carry on. He will instantly light up your life. It won't be such a bad thing having your Baby as young as you are, you may feel that you have come to the end of your life but it is only just beginning. It won't be easy and it certainly won't be all plain sailing the waters may get very rough and you will have your heart broken but while you have the love of your Son you will not want for anything else. You will grow up together and share a very special bond. You will work hard for the want of a better life and you will be successful. Don't worry about the materialistic things in life as this doesn't matter, there are far more important things, and your life will be rich in other ways.

Stand tall; be proud of your achievements and of who you are.

Petra, aged 41

Dear Sophie (19 years old)

You don't realise how much you will love the two boys you will have, but you will love them so much, don't worry about not having enough love for them both either. You will love them equally for different reasons.

I know you didn't plan on having children until you were 25 years old and married but things will work out for you. Right now you want to continue hairdressing but you will go into youth work and be accepted into university. It will make Granddad so, so happy! You will also build up a good relationship with your mum and feel comfortable enough to say No when you need to... so all in all things will be OK, just trust that they will be.

Love
Sophie (21 years old)

Dear Deb

So much to say and so little time.... So we'll start with the most important things – I love you. Everything will be okay.

Don't believe the negative things people say about you or internalise the way that people will treat you; you are a wonderful human being. Believe the praise that people give – they mean it!...... Think about it, would you give praise if you didn't mean it? I know it's difficult, but you will learn to do this in time.

I know you're very scared and think you can't handle this, but you will – there will be some bumps along the way, some major, some minor, but everything will work out in time. Giving birth isn't as scary as you think it will be, it will be forgotten the moment our son is born. (I'm not going to tell you his name because you haven't decided yet – it's your decision.)

When our son is born you are going to feel nothing for him – this isn't abnormal especially considering how little time you have had to get used to having him around, but stick in there – within two weeks you won't believe just how much you could love another human being.

Our family will forgive you sooner than you think and love our son more than we thought was possible.

The first two years are going to be the most difficult; our son will send you to the edge of the abyss at times, but there are people there who can help – when our son is 6 months old listen to your Health Visitor when she says 'let him scream at night' – seriously, if you do this (it will be one of the hardest things you do as a parent) you and our son will get a full nights sleep within four days.

It's not the end of your life as you think it is because of what people have told you - it's just the beginning. What they say is about their values and attitudes – you are better than that, just concentrate on being the best parent you can be, not the parent you think you should be.

You won't believe this but over the next 10 years you will learn to love yourself and know that you can achieve anything you set out to do! (By the way, you will be throwing yourself up and down mountains, out of aeroplanes and boats..... with the biggest smile on your face! – I better leave some surprises!)

Without this happening you would have never got into the work you have done and been able to give so much to so many – you will be fabulous at this work and it will give you so much in return you wouldn't believe me if I told you.

It's not just work that changes – we get married in a few years.... Don't laugh – you haven't met him yet so don't start giving your friends appraising looks! Incidentally – those 'friends' that don't stick around? Let them go – the friends you make in the future will love you and support you no matter what happens.

Our son will be clever, happy and confident and know he can achieve anything himself. He is 22 this year – he is independent, loving, generous and outgoing and a wonderful human being. He loves books the way we do and he's not afraid to take the risks we were too scared to when we were younger. We are so proud of him.

I want things to change for you now, and I can't do it and its heart breaking, but the difficulties that you will go through will shape you and make us a better person and mother.

Okay some quick advice – you won't take it, but at least I know I tried!

- Look at our son every day and understand what a miracle he is
- Grow your hair again – you look fabulous!
- In times of stress accept help – people like to help others and it doesn't reflect badly on you
- Carry on going to the gym – don't lose the joy it gives you
- Take more photographs of our son and hide them well
- Start moisturising daily as soon as possible
- Do something every day that scares you – you will find out why
- Look at our son every day and understand what a miracle he is (Yes I know I said that one twice – it's more important than you could ever know)

I have to go now and I don't want to – If I could see you I would give you the biggest hug……..

So I will end as I began. I love you. Everything will be okay.

Deb x

July 1965

Dear Stella (Aged 17),

So you're getting married in 3 weeks time, at 17, because you're pregnant; not quite what you had planned, but as you've often said 'plans don't often work out!'

Anyway you've decided, despite some doubts, getting married is the right thing to do. Adoption was an option but you were quite horrified when people (including the GP) suggested it, the thought of going through 9 months of pregnancy and then handing over the baby to strangers simply wasn't an option, although lots of people do apparently. And what would happen if you could not have any children in the future?

Abortion was seemingly out of the question, except under 'special circumstances' it is illegal and 'Back Street' operations can be very dangerous.

The family have been fairly OK with the situation, after the initial shock parents said 'well you're not the first and you won't be the last'. But you felt you had made your bed so you will have to lie on it. As the saying goes 'you want your baby to have a mum and a dad and a normal family life' (As far as that is possible)

So you dropped out of the 6th form but I expect you can study later on and have a career, teach maybe. You will only be 23 when he/she goes to school, it just means delaying things for while, and it's not the end of the world.

Hope all works out, you wanted children one day it's just bad timing - Good luck!

Stella (Aged 62)

Stella had 2 sons - Got an A Level at night school and went to university aged 26.

She has had a long and successful career working with young people.

Louise's Story - a tribute from her head teacher

8 Oct 1990 - Louise, a student in the upper 6th doing 3 A levels is pregnant. She went with a friend to John, the Deputy who has responsibility for the 6th Form to ask for advice. Her boyfriend, the baby's father, is one of our former students from an ethnic minority family. He is not able to offer much support. She has made the decision to have the baby and thinks she will have to leave home and drop out of school.

12 Oct 1990 - When Louise told her parents, their immediate reaction was to urge her to carry on with her A levels. At our Governors' meeting the governors endorsed the school support for Louise.

2 Nov 1990 - Louise came to tell me her gynaecologist says she will need to stop attending school in early February - she has a back problem and will need special care. The baby will be born by caesarean section in May 1991. I offered to tell her teachers, she seemed pleased to accept the offer. Louise has filled in her University entry forms.

1 Feb 1991 - Louise came in with her mother to see me and the college nurse about how we can help, especially in terms of keeping in touch when she stops attending regularly. We offer transport to lessons and use of the nurse's home as a base for free periods. Louise has an offer of a place at our local university for 1992.

22 April 1991 - By arrangement, Louise is the first candidate for French orals. I saw the external examiner at lunchtime - he expressed admiration for Louise and rated her as an excellent candidate.

26 April 1991 - We have news that Benjamin, 6lb 10oz, was safely delivered by caesarean the previous evening. I go to the hospital in the evening to visit - a lovely baby. Other staff will go in the next few days.

23 May 1991 - From nurse we hear that Louise's family are taking turns to look after Benjamin at night so that Louise can sleep through and be better able to concentrate on her revision.

3 June 1991 - For Louise's first written exam, she brings Benjamin in and nurse looks after him. This system will continue for the other exams, except for one when her mother can take a day off work to look after him.

15 Aug 1991 - Louise came in with Benjamin, who has grown a lot over the holiday, to collect her results, which are among the first I looked at. She will almost certainly have her university place confirmed.

In the evening I look back at the card she wrote on her return from Hospital, thanking me for the support she'd received. "I don't think I would've been able to manage without the help that I've been given. I will try very hard not to let you down in my exams. I intend to work hard to make the school (and Benjamin) proud of me."

We are Louise.

Dear Me,

3 years down the line, 3 years with a beautiful daughter.

I couldn't have imagined being here three years ago. Depressed, without a home, no idea how to provide for myself let alone another little one, stuck in an abusive relationship.

How far I've come...how far we've come!

Working part-time just completed an NVQ 3, living happily alone with my beautiful girl, in a lovely rented house with two bunnies!!

And I have to say, I'm proud of myself! I have a daughter I adore, a job I love and I have helped hundreds of mums by becoming a breastfeeding peer supporter! Becoming a mum has opened so many doors for me and has shown me the true value of life.

It can be tough at times but as a wise person (my mum) said to me "It doesn't get any easier, just different" and these differences bring new challenges and opportunities.

Don't look at this as the end but as the start of a new chapter. Becoming a mum has opened so many doors for me and has given me a focus. Make the most of each opportunity you are given and don't be afraid to ask for help.

Most of all enjoy being a mother and treasure every precious moment.

Shauna x

Finally... some more thank yous!

This project has happened with the help of a fantastic team of people who have supported the idea, the planning and the encouragement of letter writing!

Many thanks to all involved, especially Bob, Dan, Emma, Lianne, Dee, Chrissie, Katie, Santosh, Liz, Mike, diva, the PIPS team and the Teenage Pregnancy and Parents Champions at Connexions Leicester Shire.

And a big thank you again to all of our letter writers! I am so grateful that each of you took the time and effort to contribute to this amazing book. Your openness and honesty have made this into a powerful tool that will provide reassurance and inspiration to pregnant teenagers and young mums and dads. It is testimony to the strength and determination of young parents.

So, thank you! Sue, Dee, Jo, Katie, Suzanne, Suzi, Anne-Marie, Beverley, Casey, Camilla, Charlene, Clair, Daina, Carolyn, David, Grace, Hannah, Jade, Maria, Sara, Trish, Linnet, Steve, Ellie, Emily, Hayley, Joelle, Kathryn, Kealey, Jenny, Lianne, Lucy, Marie, Petra, Sophie, Deb, Stella, Louise and Shauna.

Vicki Smith
Teenage Pregnancy and Parents Co-ordinator
Connexions Leicester Shire